The ENGLISH COLLECTION

GW01551383

MAKING ADVERTS

Chris Davies

LONGMAN

CONTENTS

To the pupil:

This series is for your pleasure and your profit. It's like a do-it-yourself kit – but with clear instructions.

Our main hope for the series is that you enjoy doing the reading, writing, talking and listening it involves. This has been an important consideration in choosing material. But, of course, we also need to help you fulfil the requirements of GCSE and the National Curriculum. The range of work will give you opportunities to develop your ability in every aspect of English, including assessment of your own progress – watch for the 'Look Back' headings in each section.

We want you to make – to create for yourself –
  stories
  poems
  advertisements
  magazine articles
  letters
  plays –
a full variety of styles of writing.

Each book in this series takes you carefully through the creation process, working individually, in small groups or as a complete class, helping you to –
  prepare,
  discuss,
  develop ideas,
  plan,
  redraft –
so that your final pieces are presented with clarity and care.

At the same time, you will be showing your ability to read –
  fiction
  non-fiction
  between the lines
  with discrimination
  aloud or silently.

You will be talking to different people in different situations –
  your classmates
  your teachers
  members of your community.

You will show that you understand that speech varies with context, and that you can listen sensitively and with comprehension to a variety of people.

READING, WRITING, SPEAKING and LISTENING – these are the three main aspects of the National Curriculum. The English Collection will help you make the most of your ability in each of them.

✐ indicates a piece of writing

✐ indicates oral work

Speaking and listening

Pupils should be given opportunities to:

- consider language appropriate to situation, topic and purpose
- discuss issues in small groups, taking account of the views of others, and negotiating a consensus
- prepare presentations
- produce assignments where specific outcomes are required
- use audio and/or video recorders, radio, television and computer, where appropriate
- reflect on their own effectiveness in the use of the spoken word
- report and summarise in a range of contexts
- discuss increasingly complex issues
- ask increasingly precise or detailed questions
- discriminate between fact and opinion, and between relevance and irrelevance, and recognise bias

Reading

Pupils should be given opportunities to:

- consider the purpose, effect and intended audience of a range of media texts
- find and select information for themselves, and use it effectively
- read and deduce authorial points of view in persuasive writing e.g. advertisements
- quote accurately from a text to support their opinions
- recognise persuasive or rhetorical techniques
- evaluate material and draw it together coherently
- discuss the use of grammatical deviance for special effect e.g. in advertisements

Writing

Pupils should be given opportunities to:

- draft, redraft and proof-read their writing
- write advertisements
- write for a wider range of communicative or informative purposes, including: describing, explaining, reporting, expressing a point of view, persuading, comparing and contrasting ideas, arguing for different points of view
- learn how to organise and express their meaning appropriately not only for specified audiences but also for unknown audiences

1

THINKING ABOUT ADVERTS

In this section you will be thinking about how adverts work, and about what adverts are trying to do.

We are all familiar with adverts. It's obvious what they're up to – and sometimes, when you're discussing them, you've got to say things that might seem very obvious.

That's when you discover how complicated adverts really are.

✏️ Look at the advertisement on the next page. Look at it very closely – look at the picture, read the words, think about what it says and what it doesn't say. Then write down your thoughts about the questions below.

Write as much as you can – don't be afraid of stating the obvious.

1 How can you tell that this is an advertisement – rather than just a page from a magazine article?

2 What kind of readers is this advertisement talking to? How do you know?

3 What's the baby got to do with the advert? What general impression does the picture create? How is the baby meant to make you *feel* about the product? How does the text (the words) explain the presence of the baby?

4 What's meant to be good about the product? What's special about it?

5 Is this a wicked advert, a harmless advert, or a positively helpful contribution to making a better world?

6 Is it a *good* advert – an *effective* advert? Would it make you buy these batteries? Will it convince the people it's aimed at?

Environment-friendlier batteries from Varta. Europe's largest manufacturer is thinking small.

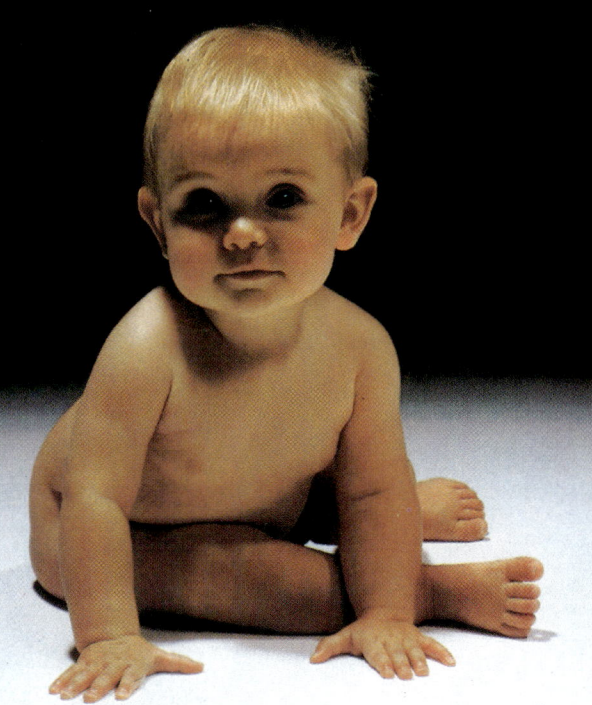

Last year, Britain dumped 48 tons of mercury contained in batteries. At Varta, this statistic weighed heavy on our minds. So much so, that we devoted ourselves to producing Britain's first mercury and cadmium-free battery, now stocked in major supermarkets.

It's only a start in cleaning up the environment. But one day our children might appreciate the first small steps taken by their parents.

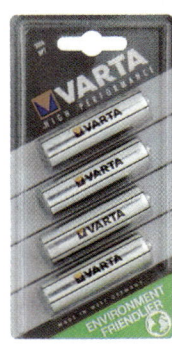

 **VARTA** ENVIRONMENT-FRIENDLIER BATTERIES

"Dances with life...
a winning performance from
Hippolyte Girardot"
Geoff Brown, THE TIMES

"Excellent feature debut...stylishly
shot...unalloyed pleasure"
Geoff Andrew, TIME OUT

"Widely and deservedly praised"
THE LISTENER

A WORLD
WITHOUT PITY

UN MONDE SANS PITIE

A film by
ERIC ROCHANT
starring

HIPPOLYTE GIRARDOT   MIREILLE PERRIER

"Impressive debut...
very engaging performance
from Hippolyte Girardot"
Barry Norman, FILM 90

"Eric Rochant's
wry tragi-comedy...
an assured debut"
Hugo Davenport, DAILY TELEGRAPH

An Artificial Eye Release

NOW SHOWING RENOIR BRUNSWICK SQ.WC1
RUSSELL SQUARE TUBE
PHONE 071.8378402 2.00 4.15 6.30 8.50

Excess Charge   pg certificate

This latest Spider O'Donovan movie is a real disaster. The plot – about the love affair between an unemployed ex-traffic warden and her probation officer (played by Spider with a quite extraordinary Scandinavian accent) – is merely unbelievable. Hayley Thurston, as the woman, is memorable mainly for the way she hands out parking tickets in the opening sequence of the film – she shows a real talent for the job, and one wonders why she ever thought of acting at all. The love scenes are quite hilarious, unfortunately.

This film is just awful – it's the most boring, incompetent and brainless waste of two hours I have ever spent in the cinema. I've never seen anything like it.

A really clever advertiser could turn a dreadful review like this into an advert for the movie *Excess Charge* – by taking certain words and phrases out of it so that they look like they mean something quite different. For instance: 'Spider O'Donovan is quite extraordinary!'

Turn this newspaper review into an advert for the movie *Excess Charge*. Pick out any words or phrases that *could* be used in an advert in order to promote this movie. You could make your advert look like the one on page 8.

There are some phrases in the film review which really couldn't be used to advertise *Excess Charge*. They're just too rude about the film for that.

Pick out five phrases from the review that make it quite clear that the reviewer thinks this is a really bad film. Once you've done that, see if it's possible to make an advert for *Excess Charge* that uses these rude phrases. Can it be done?

What does this tell us about adverts? We all know what adverts are up to: adverts can only tell us how *good* something is.

Advertisers are paid to tell us that a product is good

When we look at an advert, we know what's going on. We know that somebody is trying to sell us something – so we know that we're not going to find out what the advertisers really think about a product, about whether they like it or not. We know that advertisers are never going to say: 'We've had a good look at this product, and we have to tell you it's rubbish!' That's the one thing they can never say – because that's not what they're paid to say. Advertisers are paid to tell us that a product is good.

We all know these things about adverts – but that doesn't stop us watching them, listening to them, reading them, thinking about them. Even though we know that every advert is trying to sell us something, or make us do something, we still think: 'Okay, I know what's going on here. But I'll watch anyway.' Because . . .

. . . We like adverts

What adverts do you like?

Chat about TV adverts for five minutes (as a class, or in a group of about five people):

1 Talk about the best adverts that are on TV at the moment – talk about the ones you like best, and why.
2 Talk about the worst adverts that are on TV at the moment – talk about the ones you can't stand, and why.

➤ Draw out a chart like this, and as the conversation goes on, note down the adverts that get mentioned, and the reasons for choosing them:

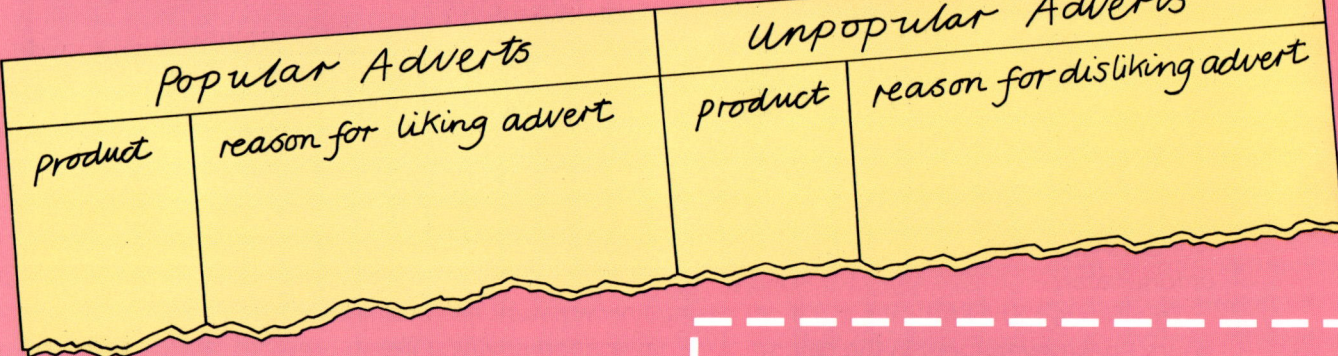

Popular Adverts		Unpopular Adverts	
product	reason for liking advert	product	reason for disliking advert

Once people start to talk about TV adverts, it's often hard to stop them. Adverts fascinate people – we all love talking about them. Why? Look at the list of possible reasons why we all watch adverts – even though we know what they're up to – and decide which reasons you think are most true.

➤ Think about which of these statements you agree with – discuss them with each other. You can write down the numbers of the different reasons under one or other of the following three columns:

very true	possibly true	not true at all

1 Adverts are on TV all the time – we can't avoid them.
2 Adverts give us useful information about things we need.
3 The music in adverts is good.
4 Adverts are often more enjoyable than the programmes they interrupt.
5 Adverts give us things to dream about.
6 Adverts help us to find ways of spending our money.
7 It's fun to say the slogans, or sing the songs, that we hear in adverts.
8 We can see the kind of life we'd like to lead in adverts.
9 Adverts are intriguing – you have to watch them carefully to find out what's going on.
10 Adverts are often very funny.
11 TV has taught us to enjoy things that happen fast – and things happen very fast in adverts.
12 Adverts help us to choose the best products.
13 It's fun to laugh at bad adverts.
14 Human beings are greedy – we always want more things than we need.
15 Advertisers use secret methods on us – we don't know why we watch adverts.
16 We're too stupid to realise what advertisers are up to.
17 Adverts are part of popular culture – something to talk about and share with other people.
18 The people in adverts are very good-looking.
19 Most adverts end too soon – we can't resist watching the next one.
20 We want to make sure we own the things that everyone else has.

2

THE BASIC TRICKS OF ADVERTISING

—

What are the most obvious tricks of advertising? What are the most straightforward methods that advertisers use to make ordinary, even boring, products look *special*?

Adjectives are the most important part of speech for advertisers. Adjectives describe things, objects, products – in advertisements, adjectives describe nouns by telling you how *good* they are.

These are some of the most popular advertising adjectives:

good/better/best free fresh delicious full sure clean wonderful special crisp safe fine big great real easy bright extra rich golden NEW

As well as using certain *basic* words like those adjectives, advertisers like to attract the attention and interest of consumers by using words in odd ways:

1 by making up new words: **flavoursome, orangemostest;**
2 by making up compound adjectives (joining two words together to make a new adjective): **environment-friendly, potato-full, creamy-soft, skin-tingling, tongue-tempting**;
3 by spelling ordinary words in unusual ways: **Beanz Meanz Heinz.**

Invent a compound adjective for each of the three simple products below. This will become the brand new advertising word that will make consumers think of the product each time they hear it. You need to make up a new compound adjective that reflects one or more of the qualities that the manufacturers believe make that product special:

Advertisers use beautiful women – and, in recent years, men as well – in various way, most often, merely to make people *look* at the advert in the first place. The advert could be for cars, vacuum cleaners or meat paste – things that have nothing to do with looking attractive at all.

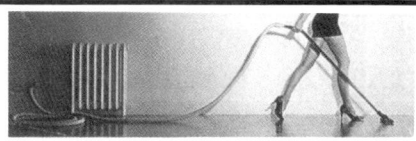

One giant step for womankind.

THE ADVERTISERS' MEETING
'What we got?'
'An ad for the InterVac Integral Vacuum System.'
'*Got* to be dynamic – *got* to appeal to women.'
'How about "One Giant Step for Womankind"?'
'Great! And we can show a woman *stepping*.'
'Let's put her in a mini and stilettos.'
'Goes without saying.'

Scope Features, Foto Theme

product	special qualities
baked bean pizza chews	popular with kids, convenient, fun
battery-driven car	quiet, economical, easy-to-drive, non-polluting
disposable tooth-brush	use and throw away, pre-toothpasted, hygienic

I love discovering new Delights

New from Delight – a range of four lean meat patés. Brussels Paté. Ardennes Paté. Bavarian Liver Paté.

Bavarian Liver Paté with herbs. Made with lean meat so they have all the taste

but less fat.

Delight: The pleasure is mine

52

Advertisers use good-looking people for two additional reasons.

1 To associate the use of a particular product with a glamorous, romantic or even sexy way of life – not actually suggesting that the product will help you find a glamorous partner, but definitely suggesting that the product brings a little glamour into your life.

2 To suggest that products to do with appearance – like shampoo, skin cream, make-up – will really make you beautiful, and sexy.

Try to find examples of these two basic tricks of advertising:

from magazines: cut out good examples of glossy adverts;
from TV: note down or record TV adverts.

Show how the adverts:

use language in a typical advertising way;
use good-looking people in any of the ways suggested.

Can you think of any other basic tricks of advertising? Discuss this with each other, and see if you can find either a magazine or TV advert that illustrates this trick.

Adverts use popular culture

Adverts are very quick – in 30 or 40 seconds, they have to influence our minds. They need to use images and sounds and situations we can recognise quickly to do this.

Adverts refer to – they quote from – things we all know about. Things like old movies, popular TV shows, pop music, famous pictures: the things that make up our *popular culture*. Advertising can only work if it can use a familiar language – the language of our popular culture.

What things are part of our popular culture?

Popular culture is made up of all the things we've enjoyed in the past: old pop music like the Beatles or the Sex Pistols; old movies like *Casablanca*, more recent movies like the Rocky films or *Dirty Dancing*; even old adverts, like the Bisto kids;
and things we enjoy in the present, that are so up-to-date that we can't name them here because they'll be out-of-date by the time you read this book.

What is your popular culture database?

A *database* is a way of using a computer to store lots and lots of information. It's an information bank. It's something that can be drawn on, referred to, whenever necessary.

Think of all the stories you've heard;
TV and films you've seen;
books, magazines, newspapers you've read;
music and radio you've heard;
major news events, and sporting events you remember;
adverts that have stuck in your mind.

It's all in there somewhere, in your memory stores, as part of your database – it's hard to remember everything, but you can probably recall quite a lot of it.

Try to make a list of some of the things that are in your database – some of the things that advertisers know that you know about – because it's their job to know about these things. Choose the things that first come to your mind:

recent movies like *Dick Tracy* and *Dirty Dancing*, or old movies like *Gone with the Wind* or *Casablanca*;
music like the first Madonna hits, Michael Jackson;
fashion movements like Punk;
events like the Falklands War, or – more recently – the revolutions in eastern Europe, the Gulf War;
TV shows like *Bread*, *Minder*, *EastEnders*, *Spitting Image*, *Twin Peaks*;
stars like Sylvester Stallone, Marilyn Monroe, Tom Cruise;
adverts like the Oxo family one.

1 First, note down as many things like that as you can remember, very quickly.
2 Then, organise these things under different headings, such as Movies/TV/Events/Adverts. After each one, write a few words describing what you most remember about that things. For example:
Movies *Dirty Dancing*
the bit I remember most of all is when the girl is learning to dance properly, and they end up in the lake together

Take your time over this and write down as much of your popular culture database as you possibly can.

How is popular culture used in the advert on page 15?

Watch a selection of TV adverts, and see if you can spot any that refer to any well-known TV shows, cinema films, or major events. Also see how many adverts you can spot which use well-known pop music in the advert. Put together a list of all adverts which make some kind of reference to the popular culture which everyone shares. You can use the following headings to list any examples you can find:

product	film or TV show quoted from	music used

CYPRUS. THE CLASSIC WINTER HOLIDAY.

TWO YEARS BEFORE THE MAST

FAR FROM THE MADDING CROWD

THREE MEN IN A BOAT

ALICE IN WONDERLAND

AS YOU LIKE IT

Cyprus offers all the ingredients to create a truly classic winter holiday.

The island is blessed with sunshine for no less than 340 days in every year.

Only in Cyprus can you ski down snow-covered mountains in the morning and laze on golden sands in the afternoon.

Try walking through the beautiful forests of the Troodos mountains or wander around Byzantine churches, Greco-Roman theatres and Crusader castles.

Work up an appetite for a traditional Cyprus meze, a meal of classic proportions, and sample local specialities like lountza, a marinated smoked ham, or tava, a delicious lamb casserole.

Enjoy the varied nightlife from intimate tavernas to international discotheques before you retire to one of our superb quality hotels or hotel apartments.

And relax in the knowledge that some things never change.

The prices remain some of the lowest in Europe, (car hire is inexpensive and we still drive on the left).

Almost everyone speaks English and you'll find the welcome is the warmest in the Mediterranean.

Especially in Winter.

Cyprus Airways

TENDER IS THE NIGHT

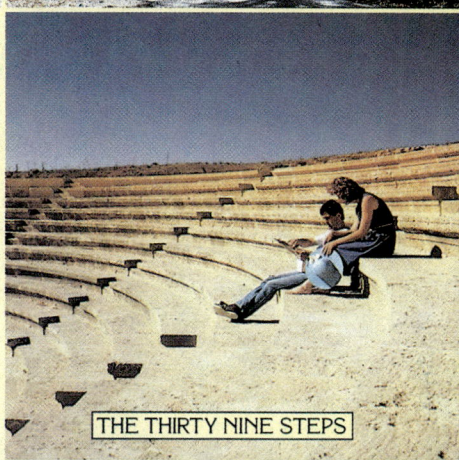

THE THIRTY NINE STEPS

WUTHERING HEIGHTS

Please send me details about Winter in Cyprus.

Name _____

Address _____

_____

_____
                                    RT 10/90

Send to: Cyprus Tourism Organisation,
213 Regent Street, London W1R 8DA
Tel: 071-734 9822/2593. Fax: 071-287 6534

☀ CYPRUS

THE WARMEST WELCOME IN THE MEDITERRANEAN

3

TRENDS AND FASHIONS IN ADVERTISING

—

Advertisers try to understand *current trends* in society – issues that are considered important by most people at a particular time, like the environment, or changing attitudes like the role of men as caring fathers.

Once they know what issues ordinary people think are important at the moment, advertisers use them in adverts (like the Varta advert on page 7). They don't always get it right. But when adverts do work, it's usually because the advertisers have spotted the things that people think are important at the time.

Are you a Superbrat?

The following newspaper article shows you how one advertising agency sees people in your age group right now.

1 What kind of young people does this report describe?
2 Do you believe this report? Are young people really like this? Do you think that the report is correct about this new generation of superbrats?
3 What kind of adverts can you imagine finding on TV in ten years time, if this report is true?

✍ Write an article of your own, in reply to the one from the *Sunday Times*. Discuss the things that the report says, and say what you think of them. You might agree, or disagree. Say what you think.

16

Enter superbrats – the children of the 1990s

A worrying vision of young people coming of age in the 1990s is contained in a report entitled "Spoilt Brats", to be published this week by Gold Greenless Trott, a leading advertising agency.

An 18-month research project has concluded that parents are living in "an idealised dream world" if they believe the new generation will adopt the caring, sharing values predicted for the decade ahead.

The findings will be sent to the advertising agency's clients as a basis for a review of marketing. They include Cadbury-Schweppes, Watney Mann and Truman, the brewers, and the Post Office; government departments will also scrutinise the trends.

Neil Cassie, the senior executive responsible for the new study, said the nation was on the brink of a teenage revolt. "The youth of today are getting very tired of listening to middle-class views and 30-something values," he said.

The fad for advertisements featuring parenthood, babies and environment-friendly life-styles will quickly give way to a return to the hard-sell approach, the report says.

People aged 15 to 24 in 1995 will be the most materialistic and affluent generation in the nation's history, according to the results of interviews with a representative cross-section of 327 children aged 12 to 15.

A growing obsession with material success, encouraged by their parents' love for the designer furniture and gadgets of the 1980s, will be inherited by young people.

Already today's children are demanding rack hi-fi systems and television sets from the age of 10; by the time they are 12, they possess the material luxuries for which many adults had to wait until they were at least 30.

More than half the boys interviewed want to have more money than their parents; a similar proportion (49%) of both sexes agreed that "looking after number one" was the correct attitude to life. Careers were more important than having children for three in four girls.

For a spoilt brat, babies bring hassle and expense. As one precocious boy told researchers: "My parents never had much money because they were always having to spend it on clothes and things for me and my brother. I don't want that. If you don't have money you can't have fun."

When it came to employment, more than half (57%) of the children interviewed said they expected finding their first job would be difficult.

However, they are wrong, "When the time comes, they will hardly have to lift a finger," says the report. It emphasises that employers will be competing to take them on.

The demographic time bomb means there will be a million fewer workers under 24 by the mid-1990s. Getting an education and finding a lucrative career will be far easier for the brats than their yuppie forebears.

Environmental issues, dangers from aerosols, food additives and agricultural chemicals are dismissed as middle-aged concerns. "If green is an issue championed by parents, young people will automatically reject it or find ways of perverting it," the report says.

Ageism itself will become a problem, with old people regarded as targets for ridicule.

By the year 2020, a generation of children – "more screwed up than any generation before them" – will have grown up and assumed positions of power, the report says. By then, the brats will be unbeatable.

Sunday Times, 14 January 1990

The article on page 17 claimed that the next fashion in advertising will be for making adverts that appeal to greed and selfishness. The following article, which also reflects the opinions of advertisers suggests exactly the *opposite*.

What kinds of advertising are predicted in the article on page 19? Pick out four or five things that you might expect to find in adverts in five years' time.

LOOK BACK

Look back over the different kinds of things that you've found out about advertising in the first three sections of this book:

1 adverts can only tell us how good something is;
2 we like adverts;
3 the basic tricks of advertising;
4 adverts use popular culture;
5 trends and fashions in advertising.

Find at least one magazine advert or TV advert which you think could be used to illustrate what each of those five ways of thinking about adverts are saying. You could present your work like the example below.

Making Adverts – part 1, Look Back

1 adverts can only tell us how GOOD something is.

example: advert for latest single from BROS.

comments: despite the fact that everyone I know HATES this record, the advert says that it is absolutely brilliant. This certainly illustrates the fact that someone has to be paid to say how good some things are.

He knows his priorities because he's looking after his kid in the metropolis . . . the Volkswagen advertisement for the 1990s

Carers and sharers

Alex Garrett on changing the face of advertising for the 1990s

A LITTLE girl is led through the mean streets of Manhattan clinging to the protective hand of her father. Suddenly, a car pulls up at the sidewalk: it is her mother, come to pick up the family.

This, the new commercial in a £3 million campaign for Volkswagen's Passat saloon car, is one of the first ads to exploit the more caring values that advertising will portray in the 1990s. As well as happy families, we can expect to see more old people grace the screens, alongside powerful businesswomen, multilingual Europeans, and people who do not look like fashion models. After a decade of paper-thin stereotypes, the advertising business is likely to come up with more believable characters.

The 1980s, a decade dominated by style and material aspirations, gave us role models to match. Nick Kamen's striptease in the Levi's "Launderette" commercial opened the way for male sex symbols in advertising, while the British Airways "Red Eye" ad showed scheming business executives at their most Machiavellian.

Women were granted a new independence, which in Volkswagen's "Changes" commercial meant throwing away the fur coat, and everything but the keys to the car.

By the end of the 1980s, with the environment suddenly established as the most potent issue on the political agenda, advertising was already having to re-evaluate the images it draws upon. The VW Passat commercial — which reverses the traditional male and female roles in car advertising — exemplifies the shift in values which places family and environment ahead of sex appeal and power. Nick Fox, account director at the agency which made the ad, BMP DDB Needham, says: "It shows a guy who has got his priorities right. He is part of New York, but he knows his priorities because he's looking after his kid in the metropolis, in the jungle."

There is already an emerging picture of the characters that advertising will portray in the 1990s.

Tim Delaney, chairman, Leagas Delaney:

It will be all about middle-aged middle England; they will be by far the biggest group of consumers in the 1990s. The population shifts will be quite dramatic and there will be tax changes and inheritance, with people inheriting houses from their parents which are worth large sums of money.

You will see older women, as we've already seen in the Revlon ads and we may have stereotyped glamour 40-45 year-olds. There will also be a "hard Green" type of person — a money-grabbing ecologist. They will all be about caring, but not sharing. We'll probably see European Man — he'll be multilingual and we could have an ad with him speaking two languages.

John Hegarty, creative director, Bartle Bogle Hegarty:

The obvious one will be caring fathers: that has already begun to be exploited, with magazines using a father and child on their cover, for example. You'll see the man doing more at home, and I think the greener image will manifest itself generally in caring and going back to the family. I think children will be a big feature, endorsing a product and engendering a feeling of well-being.

More women will be working, so the independent woman will also be a role model we'll be coming up against.

Alfredo Marcantonio, deputy chairman, WCRS/MM:

I think antiques are going to be very important in the 1990s. I think people will want anything old, old watches, old pens: it's part of the caring thing, looking after old things. You're going to have the Sixties generation in their 50s, many of the people who were hippies popping pills then will become grandparents. You could see something like the Heinz soup commercial with the old grandad, only this time he's talking to his grandson about what it was like at Woodstock. I think we'll see the child-as-fashion-accessory become a big thing. In Italy Armani sells First Communion suits, and we'll see a similar thing develop here.

Axel Chaldecott, creative partner, Howell Henry Chaldecott Lury:

I think that "realism" will be important in the 1990s. A lot of the advertising we've seen so far has been fiction, fantasy, exaggerated, entertaining. Advertising to stand out will have to be much more idiosyncratic — like the Guinness advertising. Ugliness will be exploited, because ugly people are more individualistic.

I'd like to think that old people will be treated with the realism and naturalness that they deserve, because it's terrible if they're done in a patronising way. There will be fewer "role models" because copying won't be enough anymore.

4

THE BUSINESS OF ADVERTISING

—

We all know a lot about adverts, because we see them all the time. What we don't know so much about is the kind of people who make adverts, and the different kinds of jobs they do in the process of making adverts. This section will tell you a lot about these things. It looks at the business of advertising.

The admen

These are advertising men. They are often known as *admen* – even though a lot of women are also successful advertisers. They can earn a lot of money very quickly, if things go well. The highest paid adman in the country, according to one newspaper, earns £300,000 a year.

It's their business – the advertising business – to make people like you spend your money on products you didn't even know you wanted. They need to know all about you: about the things you like, about the life you lead, about what you think and what you want. That's what they do for a living.

MOST-DESIRED CLIENTS

Cars: particularly upmarket brands like Audi, BMW and Porsche, ie the kind of cars admen like to drive. Car accounts have the advantage that they invariably spend pots of money and allow you to make commercials on location in exotic places.

Beers: lager ads are considered a creative challenge since the products are indistinguishable. Consumers admit they buy the advertising rather than the product. They provide good practice for creatives who fancy themselves as comedians: hence the ads for Heineken, Harp and Molson.

EDUCATION

Although most top admen are surprisingly intelligent – the competition is too tough for dullards to succeed – one survey found little more than a third of top agency directors were graduates.

The percentage at lower levels is undoubtedly higher, but advertising remains one of the few careers in which one can reach the heights without a formal higher education.

AGE

Youth is no bar to success in advertising. It is not extraordinary to find leading directors of multi-million pound agencies still in their late twenties.

SALARIES

Admen annoy their clients in all sorts of ways, but money is a particularly sore point. One rule of thumb is that good creative types earn their weight in gold – more, even, than the chairman or managing director of an agency. The currency was set in the early Eighties when Saatchi & Saatchi 'creative' Geoff Seymour became the first adman to receive a £100,000 salary. Within days, every self-respecting creative in town was demanding a 'Seymour', as it became known.

Mike Cozens, hired by Grey Advertising from Bartle Bogle Hegarty to be its creative director earlier last year, set new heights for hyperbole. His salary was rumoured to be a staggering £300,000, topped with a £100,000 'signing on' fee.

The manufacturer

Admen are hired by *manufacturers* who have a product to sell. It might be a product they have been making for a long time, which isn't selling as well as it used to. It might be a brand new product, which nobody's thought of wanting before.

Manufacturers don't advertise products themselves: they hire experts to do that for them. They hire *advertising agencies*. It's an extremely expensive business – manufacturers pay out millions of pounds sometimes, to bring a product to the attention of the public – of consumers.

When it comes to the advertising process, manufacturers are the *clients* and advertising agencies are the professionals.

How many manufacturers can you name? Think of all the products that you use or see in your home, or on TV – what companies make them? Brainstorm the names of as many manufacturers as you can think of.

It is the advertising agency's task to keep the clients – the manufacturers – happy, satisfied, and making a tremendous profit. In order to do this, an advertising agency employs people with many different talents, to do many different kinds of job:

AGENCY NAMES

The more ridiculously long-winded the better. Admen argue that since it is the staff which clients hire – just as in the legal profession – then the names of the partners should form the title of the agency. But this ceased to be any justification after a spate of mergers created such tongue-twisters as Still Price Court Twivy D'Souza Lintas London, Mavity Gilmore Jaume Hill Brooks FCA, Simons Palmer Denton Clemmow & Johnson and Delaney Fletcher Slaymaker Delaney Bozell.

BRITAIN'S TOP TEN AGENCIES

	KEY ACCOUNTS	BILLINGS* £million	%CHANGE ON YEAR
SAATCHI & SAATCHI	British Airways Ariel Pampers Dixons	244	+9
J. WALTER THOMPSON	Persil Oxo Kellogg's Cornflakes Polo Mints	192	+5
BSB DORLAND	Woolworth Rover	168	+4
D'ARCY MASIUS BENTON & BOWLES	Mars Bars Bisto Royal Mail Whiskas	167	+18
OGILVY & MATHER	Ford American Express	153	+19
BMP DDB NEEDHAM	Courage Volkswagen	125	-6
YOUNG & RUBICAM	British Gas Kodak	116	+25
LOWE HOWARD-SPINK	Heineken Vauxhall	105	+6
COLLETT DICKENSON PEARCE	Hamlet Cigars Barclaycard Water privatisation	97	+37
McCANN-ERICKSON	Nescafé Gold Blend Coca-Cola	94	+3

Source: The Media Register. *October 1988-September 1989

An advertising agency is organised around the following tasks:

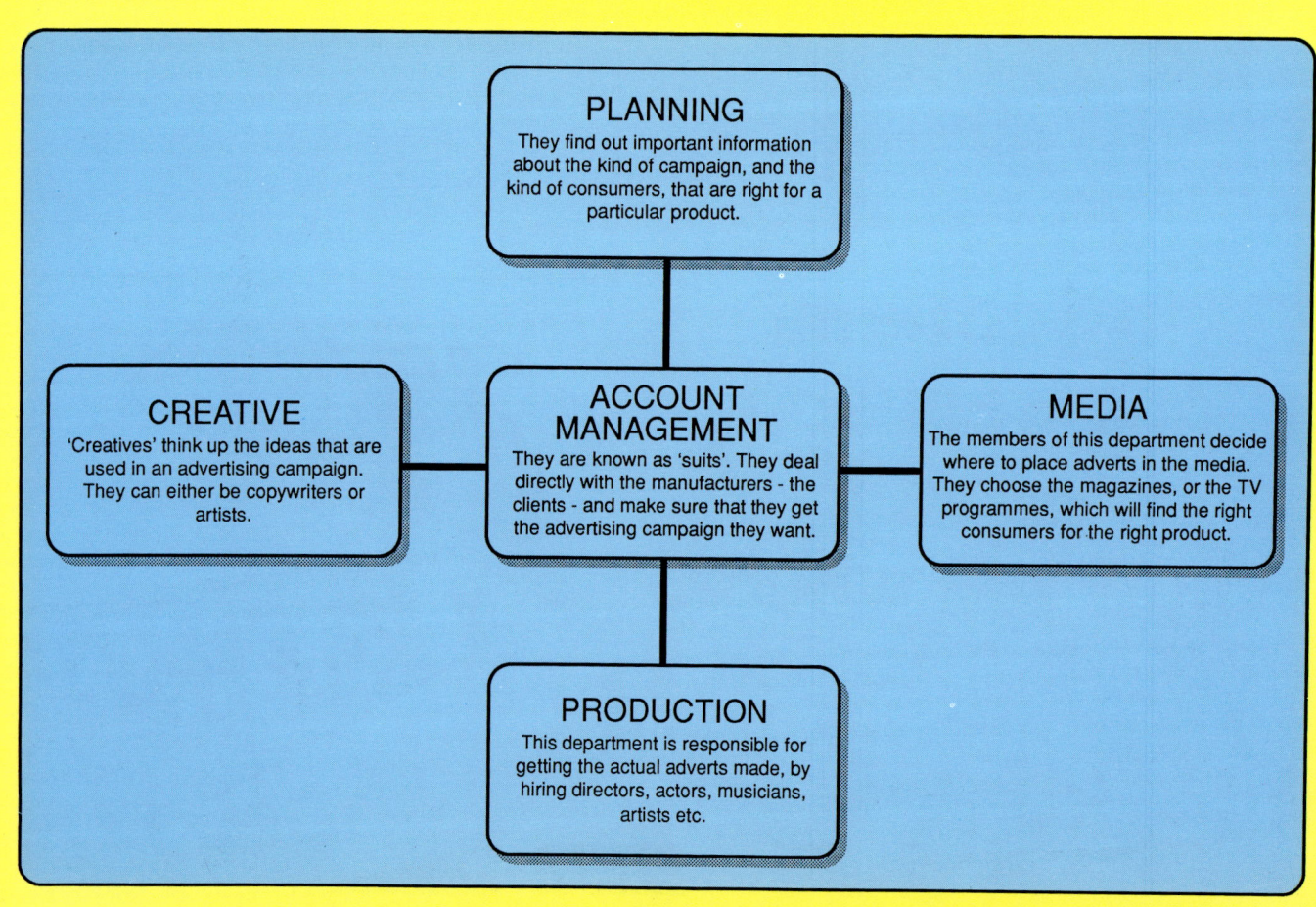

PLANNING
They find out important information about the kind of campaign, and the kind of consumers, that are right for a particular product.

CREATIVE
'Creatives' think up the ideas that are used in an advertising campaign. They can either be copywriters or artists.

ACCOUNT MANAGEMENT
They are known as 'suits'. They deal directly with the manufacturers - the clients - and make sure that they get the advertising campaign they want.

MEDIA
The members of this department decide where to place adverts in the media. They choose the magazines, or the TV programmes, which will find the right consumers for the right product.

PRODUCTION
This department is responsible for getting the actual adverts made, by hiring directors, actors, musicians, artists etc.

The planning group have to find the right consumers for a particular product. They must answer the advertising question:

Who is most likely to buy this product?

It's their job to work out the right kind of people to aim an advertising campaign at. They collect information about which section of the population is most likely to buy a particular product. This information is usually about demography, lifestyles or attitudes.

Demography

This kind of information involves putting people into categories, according to how much money they earn, the jobs they do, where they live, their ages, social class and sex. Advertisers often refer to the categories listed at the top of the next column, for instance, when choosing which part of the population to aim a particular product at.

Class A	Higher managerial, administrative, or professional
Class B	Intermediate managerial, administrative or professional
Class C1	Supervisory or clerical, and junior managerial, administrative, or professional
Class C2	Skilled manual workers
Class D	Semi and unskilled manual workers
Class E	State pensioners or widows, casual or lowest grade workers, or long-term unemployed

Advertisers often talk about a particular advert being for 'A/Bs only' or 'ClsC2s'. This helps them work out what *type* of advert will work best, and *where* to run the advert – in which newspapers, magazines, TV programmes.

Is it really possible to categorise people like this?
If you know what category people belong to, can you also guess what their habits are? As this advert from *Campaign* shows, advertisers certainly think it's possible.

If you want to pick up a 25 year old in Scotland this weekend, we can show you where.

Or a 34 year old—and all points in between—we can show you the way.

And we can guarantee that over 70% of those you talk to are ABC1s.

If you'd like to talk to a younger or older audience, we can put you in touch too.

They'll all be reading the NEW WEEKEND SCOTSMAN and LISTINGS.

The Weekend Magazine is going tabloid. Existing sections are being revamped and new subjects introduced. It's bigger and better all round.

The LISTINGS—a unique guide to what's on in Scotland—is also tabloid and is Scotland's first weekly comprehensive entertainments supplement.

Don't miss the all-new WEEKEND SCOTSMAN and LISTINGS—your ABC1s won't.

Launch issue out March 25th.

We've changed your weekend.

Contact: The Scotsman Publications, 20 North Bridge, Edinburgh. 031-225 2468, or London 01-353 0057.

THE SCOTSMAN

SCOTSMAN

WEEKEND

LISTINGS

Plus LISTINGS FULL WEEKLY GUIDE TO WHAT'S ON IN SCOTLAND

INTRODUCING SCOTLAND'S FIRST FULL WEEKLY GUIDE TO

⚡ Try this for yourselves – work out your own answers to these questions, for the two main advertising groups ABCls and C2DEs.

1 In what parts of the country, and in what kinds of houses do people from the two different groups live?
2 What different newspapers and magazines do the two groups read?
3 What different kinds of programmes do the two groups watch on TV?

Write your answers in two columns:

ABCls   C2DEs

Lifestyle

In advertising terms, a *lifestyle* means that you're the kind of person who likes to buy certain kinds of products. The things you buy show people the kind of person you are.

If you have a yuppie lifestyle, you like to buy things such as:
filofaxes
CD players
pasta makers

If you have an executive lifestyle, you like to buy things such as:
hand-made suits
swimming pools
leather golf bags

⚡ Continue each of these two lists, and decide what kinds of drink, newspapers, food, sporting goods, cars and homes people leading either of these two lifestyles might like to buy.

Once advertisers know the kinds of products that lifestyle group like to buy, they can try and convince them that the product they're advertising also belongs in that lifestyle.

⚡ How would you describe the lifestyle shown here?

Attitudes

Everyone has attitudes – their own beliefs about what matters in life. Different types of people have different attitudes.

For instance: many adverts are aimed at *mothers* (who buy most food, household goods and clothes). Advertisers are careful to make sure that any adverts for mothers emphasise the things that mothers are meant to believe in, like the advert opposite.

1 caring for the family's health;
2 keeping the family well-fed;
3 keeping the family home clean and bright;
4 keeping the family's clothes clean and bright.

The pen portrait

Once they have identified the type of consumers being targetted, advertisers try to create a detailed profile of people in this group. Young & Rubicam, a major advertising agency, instructs its employees like this:

Include a pen portrait of the consumers as individuals; bring them alive. Find out –

1 what they are really like
2 what they look like/where they live
3 what they do (work/pleasure)
4 how they view the world and their lives

➜ For instance, what kind of consumer do YOU think usually buys lager? Write a *pen portrait* of this kind of consumer, answering Young & Rubicam's four main questions in as much detail as you can.

THE VAPOUR RUB THAT'S AS GENTLE AS YOU ARE.

You can both sleep easy when you use Snufflebabe. Its vapour is so light, it can be used for babies just two weeks young, yet for all its gentleness, Snufflebabe will keep on working right through the night.

Wherever you rub Snufflebabe, on the chest, the back, or the throat, you'll have no worries about baby's tender skin.

Snuffle Babe

It's just about all a baby with a cold needs for a good nights sleep (... and mum as well).

Apart from a good night kiss.

Available from all good chemists.

MADE IN ENGLAND BY J. PICKLES & SONS. KNARESBOROUGH. NORTH YORKSHIRE.

LOOK BACK

What do you think about the way consumers are targetted by advertising agencies? Do you think they sometimes get it wrong? Find a magazine or newspaper advert where you think the agency have got it wrong, and explain why you think the targetted consumer will not buy this product.

5

THE CREATIVE WORK OF ADVERTISING

—

In this section, you will be building on what you learned in section 4, by looking more closely at the creative work of advertising. The creative group in an advertising agency are the ideas people – it's their job to think up the *idea* of a product that will make one particular group of consumers want to buy it.

USP

The main idea that the creative group must convey is the Unique Selling Point of the product. The USP is:

Either what makes a product really special – its taste, its look, its speed, its technological brilliance;
or whatever memorable idea the admen can invent in the advert to make you think that a product is different, when really it is the same as all the others. For instance, most lagers taste more or less the same. It's not information about the taste that sells lager in adverts, it's the USP that the advertisers have created – the particular, and unique, characteristic of the advert itself. For lager, this is usually something funny.

➤ Think of as many different lager adverts as you can. What is it you remember about them – what the advert tells you about the taste of the lager, or the USP that's been invented for the advert? Note down the adverts you can remember on a chart like this, in order to help you collect your thoughts:

Name of lager	What happens in the advert?	What does the advert tell you about the <u>lager</u>?	What do you think is the USP of this lager?

It makes curls curlier. It gives incredible shine. It's easy to scrunch in, easy to wash out. It's new Shockwaves Styling Wax. Use your head. Use Shockwaves.

The idea of a product

An advert is the *idea* of a product which makes consumers think about buying it. Often in adverts, you see very little of the actual product. Instead, the advert concentrates on the idea it is trying to communicate about the product:

that it is a part of a modern lifestyle, or that it provides security in the family home, or that it is the sort of thing that attractive, interesting people own, or that it is fun, or technologically advanced, or cosy like childhood.

▶ Discuss these questions:

1 What idea are you meant to get about Wella from this advert – what is the USP of this advert?
2 What kind of person is it really aimed at?

▶ Now think of at least two TV adverts of your own choice:
an advert you particularly like at the moment; and an advert that particularly annoys you.
For each advert, discuss or note down your answers to these questions:

1 What idea are you meant to get about the product in the advert – what do you think the USP of this product is?
2 What kind of person is this advert aimed at?

Appealing to the right consumers

The creative group in an advertising agency can't afford to think up ideas that *they* enjoy – a major part of their job is thinking up ideas that will appeal to one particular group of consumers – that particular part of the population which is most likely to buy the product being advertised.

The people who are creating an advert must use all the information that has been collected about the particular consumers that the product is being aimed at:

1 It must appeal to the particular *social group*, *sex*, *age group* of the consumers targetted for that campaign.
2 It must appeal to their *lifestyle*.
3 It must reflect their *attitudes*.
4 It must make use of their *popular culture database*.

The creative group – the copywriters and artists – must find ways of using the habits, beliefs, and tastes that these particular consumers are supposed to have. Try out these ideas for yourself by working on the example below.

On page 29 there are the guidelines that were given to the creative group of one advertising agency to help them plan a campaign for a well-known toothpaste. (The name of the toothpaste has been changed for this book.)

✌ In groups, study these guidelines, and discuss your answers to these questions:

1 What idea about the product must this campaign emphasise?
2 What kind of consumers will this particular campaign be aimed at?
3 What kind of taste in popular culture is this group likely to have?

✌ Create some rough ideas for an advert that will meet the requirements emphasised in the guidelines. Think up a simple situation or story for the advert which will help put over the particular idea this campaign needs to convey about Meadow toothpaste. In order to do that, it will help if you:

1 choose a well-known TV programme or movie which the likely buyers of this product might particularly like – so that you can copy it or echo it in some way;
2 choose the kind of music these consumers might like to hear in the advert;
3 think about how the people who appear in the advert ought to look – what kind of people would these consumers approve of? What kind of clothes would they wear? How would they behave?

Remember – adverts must appeal to the right consumers

Producing adverts

Once an advert has been planned and written, a rough version of it is produced, using animated drawings and a simple soundtrack. This is then tested on a sample group of consumers – and changed if necessary. Then the clients (the manufacturers) see the completed plans for the advert, and decide whether they like it. Once it has been approved, the advert is actually produced, involving directors, actors, designers, composers, musicians, film editors and so on. The most suitable media placings (the appropriate magazines, TV programmes etc.) are chosen, and the advert is finally shown.

In order to see this process in action, read through the example of an advertising campaign that begins on page 30. It's invented, but it's very much like the real thing.

Client: Meadow Product: Toothpaste	Media: T.V. 30" Requirement:	Air/Insertion date: April Budget:

Who are we talking to?

Existing users of Meadow - both those who always use us and those who keep coming back to us.
Women, particularly mothers, who feel comfortable buying and using products they know and who are not naturally experimental.
They care for those around them and identify strongly with brands which help them look after their families.

What do they think/feel about the brand?

Meadow is an archetypal family brand. Its caring image combines a strong human and approachable feeling with the virtue of family protection (which at the product level is associated with maximum fluoride protection). Despite this positive image they may worry that Meadow is no longer the best brand for looking after the family's teeth and that it is somehow less contemporary and less effective than other, newer, brands.

What do we want them to think/feel?

When I think family protection, I think Meadow.

Proposed by Account Director		Brief issue date: November 18
Accepted by Planning Director		Creative Review: November 30
		Internal Review: December 3
Accepted by Creative Director		Client Presentation: December 14
		Copy Date:

Spring Oil Incorporated, a large multinational petrol producer, has discovered that one of their petroleum by-products (zynathon-20) improves the heat qualities of wool by 250%.

It's an ideal opportunity to improve their environmental image. A new range of underwear called **Spring Thermals** will, they hope, show how interested they are in energy conservation – and people will be happier buying their petrol.

They contact a top advertising agency – Filger, Platt & Dylan (FPD) – which puts out the following memo to all its departments:

Memo to all departments of FFD from *account management* – 3/6/91

SPRING OIL ACCOUNT: **top priority**. Spring Oil is extremely image conscious, and sees an investment in underwear as helping the future sales of petroleum products. What they *really* want out of the Spring Thermals campaign is that drivers buy lots more Green Spring Hypergrade.

Take care with the *environment* line, though. Spring Oil have kept quiet about the fact that Zynathon-20, the wonder chemical which makes wool extra-hot, was actually discovered because of an industrial accident in one of Spring Oil's petroleum processing plants in Peru. The zynathon stuff was released by mistake into the atmosphere and a few thousand sheep promptly dropped dead from heatstroke. Without offending the clients, I think we should heavily DOWNPLAY the environment angle.

If we can do a good job on this one, we end up with their major petrol account. We're talking ten mill over the next three years AT LEAST. So let's really give Spring Oil something to think about – we've got TWO weeks to come up with some answers: *planning* can find out which sector of the public is most hungry for thermal underwear, and *creative* can find ways of turning all possible market sectors onto the idea of chemically enhanced longjohns.

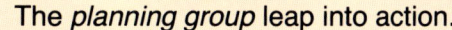

The *planning group* leap into action.

Memo to FPD account management/creative/media depts. from
FPD planning group – 12/6/91
We can identify three distinct possible target groups for
the Thermal Underwear campaign:

1 mothers with young children – C1/C2s.
Mothers in this particular social group are the most likely
to combine *spending power* and *product approval* in the
largest number (approx. 28% of overall population).

2 the "new age olds" – the new, socially aware generation of
A/B/C1s in early retirement. Restricted spending power, but
a growing market comprising 20% of the overall population,
all of which can be expected to approve strongly of any kind
of thermal underwear – A/B/C1 "new age olds" likely to be
particularly responsive to idea of environment-friendly
underwear.

3 young professionals (male & female) – A/Bs.
A small sector – 9% of the population at most – but with
virtually unlimited spending power IF they can be encouraged
to think of this brand of thermal underwear as *exclusive,*
hi-tech, extravagant & costly, fashionable & trendy.
Emphasise lifestyle associations rather than actual product.

Each of these sectors offers high profit prospects, but we
need to choose: young professionals are not going to buy any
product associated with old people – and vice versa. Mothers
tend only to buy products specifically directed at mothers.

Write a pen portrait of a typical consumer in each of these three groups.

Invent a name for a typical consumer in each of these groups, and briefly describe their appearance, age and homes.
Try to include some comments about their attitudes and beliefs – about what is important to them.

Finally, describe a typical day in the life of each person, suggesting what they might eat for breakfast, what newspaper they might read, what radio and TV they might enjoy, and what their other leisure activities might be.

The creative group have come up with some suggested campaigns. Read through each one in turn, and for each one write your own alternative suggestion for an advert to be aimed at that particular group.
Write your suggestions in the same way, in simple note-form, using the same three headings used in each case – key images, execution, slogan.

Try to provide simple sketches or illustrations to help show what *your* ideas would look like.

Outline for *thermal underwear* campaign – creative review (15/6/91)
We are ready to go with any of these three campaigns:

1. Mothers with young children (C1/C2s).
We want to suggest an idea of surrounding the family in personal warmth.

key images
warm and cosy home, happy family, safe and warm, having breakfast. Snow outside – as mother sends family out into the cold, she sounds cheerful, confident, dancing 'Spring Thermal' people out to protect them from the day ahead.

execution
animation – soft colours, soft movement: something like "Snowman" or "Grandpa" cartoon style.

slogan
"Spring Thermals surround you with protection throughout the day.
PERSONAL WARMTH GUARANTEED – IN SPRING THERMALS."

2.

the New Age Old (A/B/C1s).
We'd need to emphasise fun here — we're talking to the active old. We don't want old people to see Spring Thermals as something they need in order to survive, but something they can use to help them have fun.
Therefore, we imagine comic situations, each involving an active old person, having fun freely because of their Spring Thermals. The jokes should refer to the youth of these old people - remind them of feeling young.

<u>key images</u>
Grey, cold settings with colourful, confident old people enjoying themselves. Sense of humour - old people in rainbow-coloured Spring Thermals making fun of younger people suffering from the cold and generally taking life too seriously.

<u>execution</u>

"HE'S TENSING —
SHE'S RELAXING...
IN SPRING THERMALS"

" Spring Thermals - the secret of eternal YOUTH!!"

*Ask someone who remembers 1953 what the joke is.

3. Young Professionals (A/Bs).
This campaign will tell the story of a very stylish, very aspiring, very aware, young professional couple meeting and falling in love in a sequence of cold places.

key images
We like the idea of the North Pole for this one; ice mountains, northern lights, the ENVIRONMENT all around this couple, free in their underwear to enjoy the life they choose, together - despite the awful, awe-inspiring COLD.
The thermal underwear should look unintentionally sexy; slightly body-hugging and, at the same time, slightly loose.
A hint of sex is crucial for this group - therefore we see the adverts as being entirely about couples - particularly attractive couples.

execution
High production costs on this one; we'll have to film it in the actual Arctic. We'll need a top feature-film director for this, of course.

slogan
We want to use a different product name if we go with this one - SLOGAN: "Recycle your own body heat - feel the heat of BODYHOT."
OR "Go far, go thermal, go BODYHOT."

The whole country is going to be talking about this yuppie couple. We suspect that this might not match the corporate image that Spring Oil are after, but thermal underwear is a tricky product to sell to this market, and this idea will do the job, we reckon.

We're talking 50 megaton airburst here – in six months time, everyone who is ANYone will be talking BodyHot Thermals.

Which idea do you think will work?

Which idea do you think FPD should offer to Spring Oil?

Which one of these campaigns – including your own suggestions – do you think FPD should recommend to their clients Spring Oil?

Which one do you think Spring Oil should go for?

Which one of the three will result in a) the highest profits on the underwear itself; and b) the best company image for Spring Oil?

Which one would you most like to see yourself? Is that the best one to choose?

✍➤ Discuss this, and then write a memo from account management to the marketing department of Spring Oil, telling them about the *one* campaign idea out of the three suggestions that you prefer, and:

1 why the target consumers you've selected are the best choice;
2 why the creative ideas are suitable for that group.

Advertising is a high risk business

People who work in advertising don't operate on guesswork – they are constantly learning new things about how consumers think, what consumers want, what kinds of lives consumers live and want to live, what worked and didn't work in the last campaign.

They are constantly alert to the latest trends in popular taste, in the economy, and in social values. All these things help them figure out how to plan a campaign.

But however skilful, scientific, and professional advertisers are, no advertising campaign is sure to work.

And when a campaign doesn't work, most clients aren't going to say, 'OK, so that's £2,000,000 down the drain. Never mind.' They're going to say, 'We're taking our account to another agency.'

That's when the people in advertising stop being so smooth and confident, and find themselves having to trade in the Porsche for a Skoda.

LOOK BACK

✍➤ Advertisers spend a lot of time creating pen portraits of typical consumers – from what you have learnt in this section, write a pen portrait of a typical advertising person. Describe that person's age, sex, home, car, habits, beliefs and lifestyle.

✍▷ If you decided to apply for a job in an advertising agency, which particular job in advertising would you most like to do? What skills do you think you would most possess for this job?

Now that you have had the opportunity to think about adverts in different ways, you should understand enough about the whole process to do some advertising of your own. Before you move on to the next section, start with this warm-up exercise.

Sell your teachers

Nowadays, schools have to look after their own money – they have a certain amount of money to spend each year on everything, including teachers. And if they run out of money, they have to find ways of getting more.

Imagine a situation in which a school desperately needs an extra £50,000. That is roughly the cost of three teachers' salaries. So the school decides to sell off three of its very best teachers on the Teacher Transfer Market (just like footballers). If the school can manage to sell the contracts for three teachers to other schools, then it gets a nice transfer fee, plus it saves on the cost of their salaries.

So it advertises these teachers in the new, glossy education mag *Top Teacher*.

✍ Write the advertising copy to sell three very different teachers from this school – it will help you if you think of the three best teachers you know.

Concentrate on the USP (the Unique Selling Point) of each of these teachers. You might want to pick out a particular teacher's:

sense of humour;
good looks and brilliant dress sense;
ability to control disruptive pupils;
expert knowledge of their subject.

Your advert will be all about that USP – it's the one idea you want to get across in the advert. You want to make the people who read the advert feel that this particular USP is the one thing in the world they want to find in a teacher, and that the particular teacher you're selling actually possesses that USP. You should say far more about the USP than about the actual teacher.

Whatever USP you choose, it must be something that seems special, unique, worth buying. And remember – an advert can only say something *good* about a product.

6

MAKING RADIO ADVERTS

—

You now know quite a lot about how the business of advertising works. Here's your opportunity to put that knowledge to some practical use. In this section and in section 7, you will find suggestions for running two different kinds of advertising campaigns. Read through these suggestions, before deciding whether you want to work on the first idea (radio adverts), the second idea (a major campaign), or both.

The point of this activity is to make a radio advert that is as much like the real thing as possible – you'll include a recording of the advert, and a report of at least 1500 words about how you made that advert, in your coursework folder.

Get the picture?

What's special about radio adverts?

1 They're local

At present, all UK commercial radio stations operate locally – the overall name for this kind of broadcasting is Independent Local Radio – ILR. Therefore, most radio adverts are for local businesses: local shops, hairdressers, clubs, restaurants, transport, services etc.

2 They're inescapable

We hear radio while eating, having a bath, working, driving a car – people don't need to stop what they're doing to listen to radio. A good radio advert can make itself heard at all times of day, in all kinds of situation.

3 They only use sound

Obviously – but it's important to think about what this means: it's both the strength and weakness of radio advertising. In a radio advert, you have to convey a sense of excitement, enthusiasm, urgency – you have to make an **impact** using just:

voices
music
sound effects (on some occasions)

With only these things, you can create an *illusion* of anything on – or beyond – the earth.

4 They are easy to make

You can make a radio advert using just:

two tape-recorders
one or two voices
a carefully written script
a music tape
a sound effects tape

5 They're cheap

Because they're easy to make, radio adverts are also cheap to make – which means that it doesn't cost very much to pay for a campaign. A campaign of thirty broadcasts costs about one-tenth of what the same amount of time would cost on TV.

Look at the rate card (page 39) from Fox FM, one of the most recent ILR stations to open in the UK (1989).

You can't watch TV in the car.

You can't watch TV in the shower.

You can't watch TV in the street.

You can't watch TV whilst jogging.

Get the picture?

CAPITAL RADIO
CAPITAL RADIO 95 8FM STEREO AND CAPITAL GOLD 1548AM
The picture's better on radio.

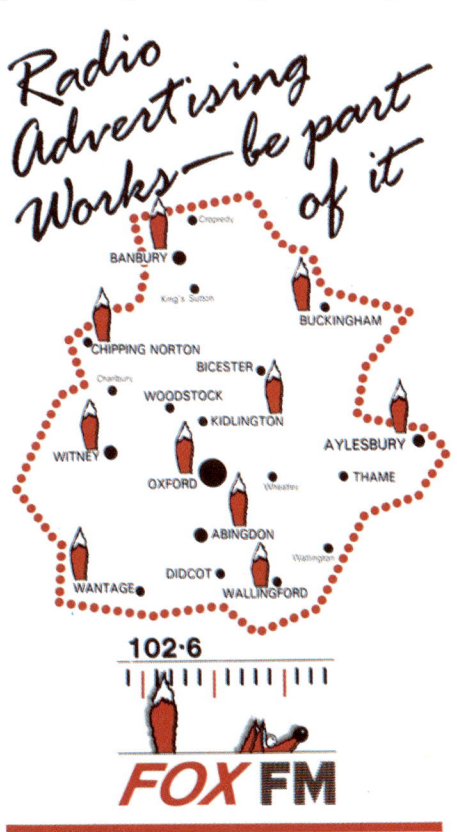

Radio Advertising Works—be part of it

102·6 FOX FM

If a high enough proportion of Fox FM's possible audience of 65,000 are to take notice of the advert and if, as Fox FM says, an advert needs to be heard at least four times before it is really noticed, then that advert needs to be broadcast about 4 times a day for at least a week if it's going to work. Look at this example:

A local furniture shop serves 1000 customers each week, resulting in a weekly profit of £4000.
It decides to spend £1000 on a short advertising campaign, which results in an extra 500 customers during the following week, earning it an extra £2000.
Then that shop has made a clear profit of £1000.

And that, in the end, is the whole purpose of advertising.

Listen to some radio adverts

➤ If you can, listen to Independent Local Radio (ILR) – 95 per cent of the UK population are supposed to be able to pick up ILR broadcasts.

1 Record a morning's broadcasting from an ILR station – try to catch as many adverts as you can. The most advertising allowed in a single hour is 9 minutes. Most radio adverts last 30 seconds.

2 List the different businesses/products you hear being advertised (but you're just going to concentrate on the local businesses).

4 Listen to the voices – listen to the way people speak. How would you describe the way they speak in each different advert? Try to find one word that sums up the tone of voice used in each advert:

cheerful? humourous? confident? smooth? excited? or what?

5 Write down at least one memorable phrase from each advert.

6 Choose at least two adverts for which you write down everything that is said – the whole script.

7 Practise saying those scripts exactly as they were delivered on the radio. Copy the tone of voice, until you can use your voice just like the professionals!

Make your own radio advert

➤ You should now be ready to make your own radio advert by following these stages.

Stage one – choose a local business

Choose a *real* local business to advertise. This can be anything you like – a local record shop, hairdresser, pizzeria, disco or football club – so long as it is the kind of business that really might advertise on local radio (but, ideally, has not actually done so).

Stage two – explain what you're up to

Arrange to talk to the people who run the local business you've chosen. Explain to them what you're up to – that you're making a radio advert as part of your GCSE coursework – and ask them if they can help you by answering a few questions. Explain that the finished product is not going to be broadcast (unless something very surprising happens!).
Try to get their answers to the following questions:

1 Is there something about their business which they think makes it special?

2 What kinds of customers mainly use their business?

3 Do they have any special offers worth mentioning?

4 What kind of impression of their business would they like a radio advert to give – fun funny funky dignified?

Stage three – write the script

Write the script for an advert for this business – the finished advert should last for exactly 30 seconds. The following guidelines will help you – but the final choice is yours, based on your ideas about what will most help to sell the business you have chosen:

1 Start with something to catch the listeners' attention, such as:
ask a question that listeners will want to find out the answer to;
say something unexpected or confusing that listeners will want to make sense of;
make a joke or use a funny voice/sound effect.
The opening is crucial. It has to *intrude* on the listeners' consciousness and distract their attention away from whatever they were doing at the time.

2 Then find a way of convincing listeners of the importance to *them* of the particular USP you've chosen – don't mention the actual business yet – just get the listeners thinking about the USP. That might be:
the *fun* of shopping in a particular shop; or
the unusually large *range* of products it offers; or
the unusually low *price*.

3 Then name the business itself, and make it clear how it provides just that USP the advert has emphasised.

4 Finally use a simple slogan or jingle to reinforce the USP, and to connect it to the name of the business. If necessary, end by making sure that listeners know where the business is, or how to get in touch with it.

Remember to decide what kind of audience your advert is aiming for;
families   housewives   young men   old people.

Don't forget a simple, memorable slogan (something spoken – '*prices for all pockets*') or a jingle (something sung – '*London is closer than you think/When you travel Oxford City Link!*'). Keep the words you choose simple, clear and lively.

Stage four – practise it

When you've written a first draft, practise reading it several times – the success of the final advert depends on you reading the words as if you really believed in them, as if you were really enthusiastic and confident about what you're saying.

Stage five – find the background music

Find the background music you want to use – this is almost always *instrumental* music (no singing).
You'll be playing this music in the background on one tape-recorder while you're talking, so that both your voice and the music are picked up by the recorder you're using for the actual advert.
Practise get the sound balance, the timing, and your own delivery just right.
Then start recording. After four or five attempts at recording, play the best version/versions to some other people, and ask them for sensible comments. Listen to any criticisms they might have about the script, the delivery, the music, or the recording.
Revise your script if necessary, and try again.

Stage six – play your advert

When you've finished the advert, play it to the people who run the business if you can, and find out what *they* think of it.
Don't forget to note down their comments.

Write a report

Review the whole experience of making a radio advert by writing a detailed report on what you did, why you did it, and what you thought about what you did. This should be a full-scale, major piece of coursework. Include:

1 an explanation of why you chose the particular local business that you advertised;
2 the information you found out about the business – what it sells, what its USP is, who its customers are;
3 all drafts of your script, with an explanation of how you tried to make the advert fit the particular needs of the business you were advertising. Say something about why you chose, or changed, the particular words you wrote for the script;
4 a description of the problems you encountered in recording the advert; what others said about the advert; what the people who own the business said about it (if possible); what you thought about it.

LOOK BACK

Conclude by talking about what you have *learned* from this exercise about the business of making adverts.

7

PLAN A MAJOR ADVERTISING CAMPAIGN

The point of this activity is to plan an advertising campaign aimed at children. After working through the various stages, you will have the skills to produce the kind of sample material real advertisers use when planning campaigns.

Aiming adverts at children

According to Young & Rubicam, a major advertising agency:

'children offer an extremely viable marketing opportunity.'

In other words: it certainly isn't a waste of time aiming adverts at children. Why is this?

1 There are a lot of them.
   In 1986, children aged 0–14 made up 19 per cent of the UK population, and that figure is expected to increase in the next few years.

2 They spend a lot of money.
   It is estimated that children in the UK aged 8–16 spend, between them, a total of £2,300,000,000 of their own money each year – that's an average of £5.69 *each* every week. They mainly spend this money on toys, snacks and confectionary products. Over 60 per cent of all *savoury snacks and crisps* sold in the UK are bought by children and young people. That's the market you are going to work on in this section.

The kind of advertising that's required

Here is some information that will help you to think about the kind of advertising that's required.

1 Children are very *brand/label* conscious. They don't like supermarket 'own' brand products (a brand is the particular make or name of a product – like 'Smiths Crisps'). Children prefer well-known brands.

2 In general, children enjoy, and therefore take a lot of notice of, adverts which use the following things:
   pace and visual action
   colour
   humour
   music (catchy tunes)
   catchphrases
   unconventionality (they don't like solemn or pompous things)
   visual effects more than words

3 But children of different ages respond differently to advertising. Children change a lot from one stage of childhood to another – their interests, enthusiasms and concerns change a lot. And boys usually have very different interests and concerns from girls. So either use *broad appeal* by making adverts work on several levels or *target* the advert very precisely at one particular childhood group.

   Make your *own* lists of things like music, hobbies and TV programmes that boys and girls of different ages enjoy.
   Try to write at least four things for boys and four things for girls in each of these age groups: 5–7; 8–11; 12–14.

4 The main differences between boys and girls, according to Young & Rubicam, are these:

   girls
   more sociable/emotional
   develop more quickly
   better verbal skills

   boys
   more physical/aggressive
   slower to grow out of childhood
   greater need to be entertained

   Do you agree with these descriptions?

Plan the campaign

Use the information about children to help you with planning a campaign: you are going to work out ideas for *repositioning/reinvigorating* (advertisers' talk for 'bring a dead product back to life, and improving its sales') a well-known children's brand of snack food (examples: crisps, peanuts, muesli bars).

Stage one – choose a product to advertise

Take a lot of care in choosing the product you will advertise. Make a list of as many real snack foods/crisps-type products as you can think of. You are looking for a product that:

1 has been around for quite a long time;
2 has a fairly well-known brand name;
3 young people in the 11–15 age group do *not* buy a lot of;
4 needs a powerful advertising campaign to bring it back to the approval/attention of young people.

It really does not matter whether the product is nice to eat or not, or whether you like it – all that matters is that it is well-known and in need of strong advertising to make it popular again.

Stage two – select a target age group

Narrow down the age group you are going to work on – 11–15 is too wide. Choose 11/12 year olds, or 13/14 year olds. This will make a big difference to the kind of advertising strategy you need to use.

Stage three – carry out market research

Investigate the popularity of the brand you have chosen by doing a quick piece of market research during the course of one dinner-hour at school. Interview some pupils in the age group you have chosen. Take care to note down and keep a record of the answers you get – you need to end up with this kind of information:

age of each person interviewed
spending power (how much own money to
   spend each week?)
boy or girl
how much snack food eaten usually
favourite snack food
opinion of the brand you have chosen to
   advertise

Stage four – plan an advertising strategy

Look at the information you have collected about the interests and enthusiasms of boys and girls in the age group you've chosen, and think about the kinds of advertising that young people enjoy, so that you create a way of making the product you've chosen look exciting in an advert.

1 What *USP* will you emphasise? Will it be a particular, real characteristic of the product (for instance 'these crisps are saltier than other crisps'), or will you need to create some emotional feature that you attach to the product (for instance 'people who eat these crisps are more naughty, and have more fun, than everyone else').

2 What *theme* will you use for the campaign? If, for instance, you are going to give the crisps a USP of naughtiness, then you could make up a kind of 'Bash Street Kids' situation for the adverts (remember that children enjoy adverts with pace, visual action, colour, humour, unconventionality).

3 What is the *popular cultural database* of these children – what are the books, films, TV, comics and music they enjoy. And how can you use any of that in the advert?

4 What *slogan/jingle* will you use in all the adverts, as the thing they remember and repeat from the adverts?

Stage five – write a first draft script

You can now have a first go at turning your ideas into a script for a TV advert for the product.
This script could be in *story-board* form (see page 45), in three columns – the first column shows a sketch of the main visual images, the second column shows the words that will be spoken, the third column shows the sounds/music that will be heard.

Stage six – check on acceptability of your ideas

Advertisements have to follow rules. All television and radio advertising is governed by the Independent Broadcasting Authority, which has quite strict rules. In addition, all other advertisements have to follow a set of rules that the advertising business itself has worked out: these rules are called *The British Code of Advertising Practice*. The basic rule in this Code – the essence of good advertising – is that: **All advertisements should be legal, decent, honest and truthful.** You could argue for quite a long time about how many advertisements are really all of those things – but advertisers really do have to try very hard to live up to that.

In particular, there are rules for all adverts aimed at children. Here are some of those rules, so that you can check the plans you have already made against them. Do your ideas break any of these rules? Does the example opposite – for Maxie Munchies – break any of these rules?

* Advertisements should not encourage children to make themselves a nuisance to their parents, or anyone else, with the aim of persuading them to buy an advertised product.
* No advertisement should cause children to believe that they will be inferior to other children, or unpopular with them, if they do not buy a particular product, or have it bought for them.
* No advertisement for a commercial product should suggest to children that, if they do not buy it and encourage others to do so, they will be failing in their duty or lacking in loyalty.
* Where the results obtainable by the use of a product are shown, these should not exaggerate what is attainable by an ordinary child.
* Children should not appear to be unattended in street scenes unless they are obviously old enough to be responsible for their own safety; they should not be shown stepping carelessly off the pavement or crossing the road without due care; in busy street scenes they should be seen to use the zebra crossings when crossing the road.
* Children should not be seen behaving dangerously, e.g. leaning far out of windows, standing on the parapets of bridges or climbing without adequate supervision or protection.
* Children should not be shown using matches or gas, paraffin, petrol or any mechanical or electrical appliance which could lead to their suffering burns, electrical shocks or other injury.

If there is anything in your script which breaks those rules, change it straightaway.

visual	words	sound-track
	**1** Schoolboy voice: "have you ever wanted to throw your teacher onto the school roof?"	playground noises laughter
	2 "Well, if you eat enough Maxie Munchies you might be able to."	sound of crunching music: chorus of naughty boys singing "We love Maxie Munchies"
	3 "but me, I've got better things to do."	"Maxie Munchies are really NAUGHTY to eat."
	4 "like eating everybody else's while they're busy getting him down again."	"the naughtier you are" sound of teacher screaming "the more you need."
	5 adult male voice, good-humoured; "Maxie Munchies – good for you BAD BOYS".	more playground noise and laughter. music repeated; "Maxie Munchies, Maxie Munchies".

Stage seven – decide on possible media placings

Where should your adverts be seen or heard? If in magazines, what magazines? If on TV, in the middle of which programmes? If on Independent Local Radio, at what time of day? You should have a pretty good idea now of what young people enjoy at different ages.
Decide where to run your advertising campaign.

Stage eight – produce your adverts

Don't be unrealistic about this – you are *not* a multi-million pound organisation. You don't have the resources to produce real adverts – but you do have the knowledge and skills to produce the kind of sample, mock-up material that real advertisers would use during the planning stage of a campaign. Try to produce some of the following material:

1 *A detailed storyboard for one TV advert or outline storyboards for a sequence of three TV adverts*. It's best to start with the TV advert because these are usually the centre of a campaign, and any other kinds of advert usually grow out of these.

2 *A radio advert*. This can be a sound-only version of the TV advert you will never actually make.

3 *A magazine advert*. This can take the main idea from the TV advert and present it in a single page picture plus words. You can use collage for this – cutting out images and words from real magazines and pasting them together. Alternatively, if you have access to a school computer with a desk-top publishing program, you can design an advert on that.

You can also put your ideas onto *video* if there is a camera available. Don't try to act out the advert – just use drawings or cut-out images from magazines pasted together, and the soundtrack (voices, music, sound effects) to give an impression of what a finished advert would be like.

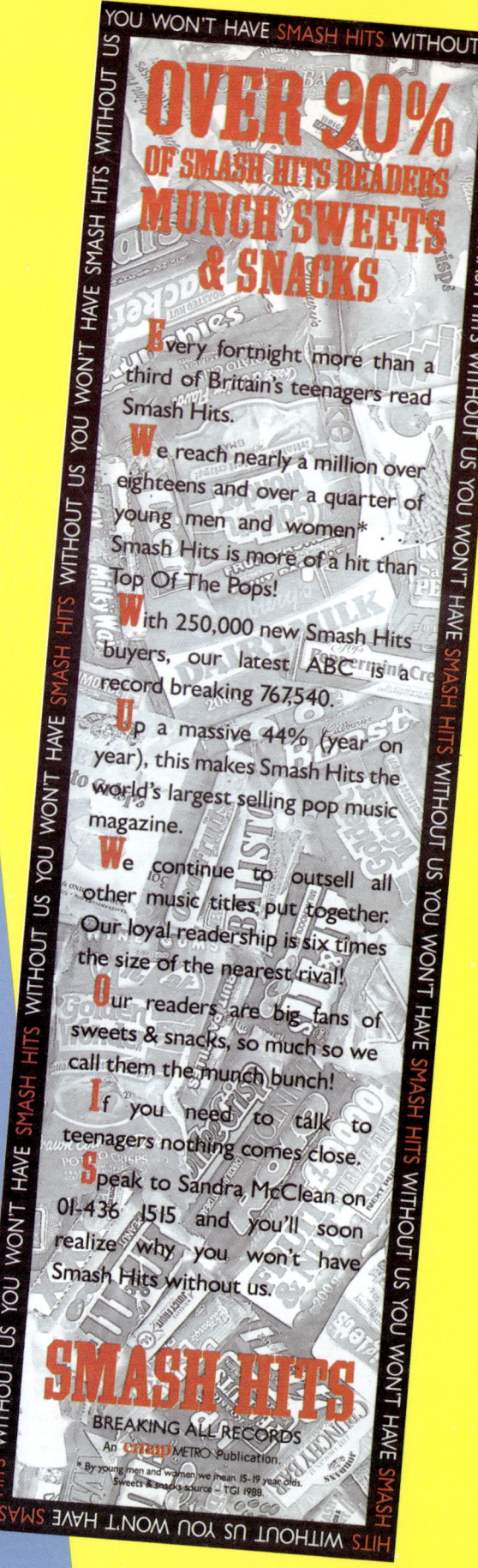

Stage nine – consumer research

Collect together a few representative members of your target group (in other words, persuade some younger pupils to come and help you during a lunch-hour) – show them the sample advertising materials you've produced, and ask them if they think they would succeed in making them feel more enthusiastic about the particular brand you have chosen. Change your adverts if you discover that they don't work with the target consumer group.

Write a report

↗ Write a report on the whole campaign, as if it was for your clients – that is, the manufacturers of the snack food you selected. Explain your ideas for this campaign, and why you think they will *reinvigorate* this particular brand in the eyes of your selected target group of consumers. Talk about:

1 the USP you've chosen;
2 the particular theme for this campaign;
3 the ways that your advert meets the requirements of the Code of Practice;
4 what the sample group of consumers thought of the adverts.

Sell your ideas to the clients – use this report to convince them that this campaign will improve the sales of their product.

And if you really think the project has gone well, send a copy of this report and of your sample materials (you need to keep the originals for your coursework folder) to the actual manufacturers. Address it to the Marketing Director, followed by the name and address of the company, which you should be able to find on the product packaging. Explain why you produced these materials (as part of your GCSE coursework) and ask them what they think of them.

LOOK BACK

The introduction to this module said that creating an advertising campaign ensured you covered all eight assessment objectives for GCSE. They are listed below. Show how each one is needed to produce a successful advert:

1 Understand and convey information.
2 Understand . . . and present facts, ideas and opinions.
3 Evaluate (judge) information in reading material.
4 Express what is felt and what is imagined.
5 Recognise implicit (below the surface) meaning and attitudes.
6 Show a sense of audience and an awareness of style in formal and informal situations.
7 Show accuracy in punctuation, spelling and sentence structure.
8 Communicate effectively and appropriately in spoken English.

Acknowledgements

We are grateful to Times Newspapers Ltd for permission to reproduce the article 'Enter superbrats – the children of the 1990s' by Rufus Olins in *Sunday Times* 14.1.90, © Times Newspapers Ltd 1990.

We are grateful to the following for permission to reproduce photographs and advertisements:

Artificial Eye, pages 2 (top), 8; Capital Radio, pages 37, 38; Coca Cola, page 21 (bottom); The *Correspondent*, pages 2 (centre), 20, 21 (top), 22; The Creative Company, pages 3 (centre), 42; Cyprus Tourism Organisation, page 15; Delight, page 13; Fox FM, page 39; The *Guardian*/BMP Needham, page 19; L A Gear/Saachi & Saachi, pages 2 (bottom), 24; Louis Marcel/Butler, Borg, Millest, Eraser Irc Limited, page 11; Nike, page 21 (bottom); J Pickles & Sons, page 25; Scope Features/Foto Theme, page 12; The *Scotsman*, page 23; Smash Hits, page 46; Varta Limited, page 7, Geoff Ward, page 3 (top), 31; Wella, page 27; Wickens, Tutt, Southgate, page 20.

Illustrations on pages 32, 33, 34 and 45 by Jane Whittingdale.
Cover illustration by Christopher Brown.
Series designed by Jenny Portlock of Pentaprism

LONGMAN GROUP UK LIMITED,
Longman House, Burnt Mill, Harlow,
Essex CM20 2JE, England
and Association Companies throughout the world.

First published 1991

ISBN 0 582 05943 7

Produced by Longman Group (FE) Ltd
Printed in Hong Kong